PIANO • VOCAL • GUITAR

MW00534355

BEST OF RED HOT CHILI PEPPERS

ISBN 0-634-02306-3

HAL•LEONARD®
CORPORATION
7777 W. BLUEMOUND RD. P.O. BOX 13819 MILWAUKEE, WI 53213

Visit Hal Leonard Online at
www.halleonard.com

BEST OF RED HOT CHILI PEPPERS

TABLE OF CONTENTS

PAGE

4	Aeroplane
11	Around the World
20	Behind the Sun
24	Breaking the Girl
42	Californication
29	Give It Away
52	Knock Me Down
58	My Friends
62	Otherside
68	Scar Tissue
80	Soul to Squeeze
73	Suck My Kiss
86	Under the Bridge
91	Warped

AEROPLANE

Words and Music by ANTHONY KIEDIS, FLEA,
CHAD SMITH and DAVID NAVARRO

It's my aer-o-plane. Pleas-ure spiked with pain.

Is my aer-o-plane.

(w/Gtr. Solo)

Play 8 times

AROUND THE WORLD

Words and Music by ANTHONY KIEDIS, FLEA,
JOHN FRUSCIANTE and CHAD SMITH

12

G7(no3rd)

G

8vb throughout

Come back, ba-by, 'cause I'd like to say I've been a-round the world, back from Bom-bay. Fox hole, love pie in your face, liv-in' in and out of a big fat suit-case. Bon-a-fide ride, step a-side my john-son. Yes I could, in the woods of Wis-con-sin. A-wake up the cake; it's a lake. She's kiss-in' me

G7(no3rd)

8vb throughout

3

G

Where you wan-na go? Who you wan-na be? A - what you wan-na do? Just come with me.

I saw God, then I ___ saw the foun-tains. You and me, girl, sit-tin' in the Swiss moun - tains.

BEHIND THE SUN

Words and Music by FLEA,
ANTHONY KIEDIS, HILLEL SLOVAK,
JACK IRONS and MICHAEL BIENHORN

BREAKING THE GIRL

Words and Music by ANTHONY KIEDIS, FLEA,
JOHN FRUSCIANTE and CHAD SMITH

Original key: G# major. This edition has been transposed down one half-step to be more playable.

CODA

GIVE IT AWAY

Words and Music by ANTHONY KIEDIS, FLEA,
JOHN FRUSCIANTE and CHAD SMITH

Funk/Rock

Give it a-way. Give it a-way. Give it a-way now. Give it a-way. Give it a-way. Give it a-way now.

Give it a-way. Give it a-way. Give it a-way now. I can't tell if I'm a king-pin or a pau-per.

Greed-y lit-tle peo-ple in a sea of dis - tress. Keep your more to re-ceive your less.

Un-im-pressed by ma-te-ri-al ex - cess. Love is free love. Me say, "Hell, yes."

Give it a-way. Give it a-way. Give it a-way now.

Give it a-way. Give it a-way. Give it a-way now.

Give it a-way. Give it a-way. Give it a-way now. Oh, oh, yeah.

Give it a-way. Give it a-way. Give it a-way now.

Give it a-way. Give it a-way. Give it a-way now.

Give it a-way. Give it a-way. Give it a-way now. I can't tell if I'm a king-pin or a pau - per.

His heart is nev-er gon-na with-er. Come on eve-ry-bod-y, time to de-liv-er.

Give it a-way. Give it a-way. Give it a-way now. Give it a-way. Give it a-way. Give it a-way now.

Give it a-way. Give it a-way. Give it a-way now. I can't tell if I'm a king-pin or a pau-per.

Em

Backwards Guitar Solo

Give it a-way now.   Give it a-way now.

Give it a-way now.   Give it a-way now.

Give it a-way now.   Give it a-way now.

Give it a-way now.   Give it a-way now.

Give it a-way now.

Give it a-way now.

Give it a-way now.

Give it a-way now.

Give it a-way now.

Give it a-way now.

Give it a-way.

CALIFORNICATION

Words and Music by ANTHONY KIEDIS, FLEA,
JOHN FRUSCIANTE and CHAD SMITH

Moderately slow

KNOCK ME DOWN

Words and Music by ANTHONY KIEDIS, FLEA,
JOHN FRUSCIANTE and CHAD SMITH

MY FRIENDS

Words and Music by ANTHONY KIEDIS, FLEA,
CHAD SMITH and DAVID NAVARRO

OTHERSIDE

Words and Music by ANTHONY KIEDIS,
FLEA, JOHN FRUSCIANTE and CHAD SMITH

SCAR TISSUE

Words and Music by ANTHONY KIEDIS, FLEA,
JOHN FRUSCIANTE and CHAD SMITH

(1., 3.) Scar tis-sue that I wish you saw. __ Sar - cas-tic mis-ter-know-it - all. __
(2.) Blood loss in a bath-room stall, __ South-ern girl with a scar-let drawl. __

Close your eyes and I'll __ kiss you 'cause __ with the birds I'll share. __
Wave good-bye to Ma __ and Pa 'cause __ with the birds I'll share. __

SUCK MY KISS

Words and Music by ANTHONY KIEDIS, FLEA,
JOHN FRUSCIANTE and CHAD SMITH

SOUL TO SQUEEZE
from the Paramount Motion Picture THE CONEHEADS

Words and Music by ANTHONY KIEDIS, FLEA,
JOHN FRUSCIANTE and CHAD SMITH

Moderately, not too fast

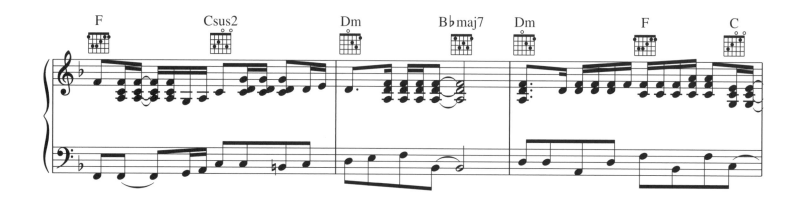

UNDER THE BRIDGE

Words and Music by ANTHONY KIEDIS, FLEA,
JOHN FRUSCIANTE and CHAD SMITH

90

WARPED

Words and Music by ANTHONY KIEDIS, FLEA,
CHAD SMITH and DAVID NAVARRO

It's up-end - ing me.

I'm pre-tend - ing, see, to be

strong and free _____ from

my de - pen - den - cy. _____

So much ___ I - love, ___ so ___ rare ___ ___ to dare, ___ a - fraid of ev - er be - ing there. ___